W9-COF-118

BEYOND
WOK

Project Editor: Lisa M. Tooker

Translator: Christie Tam

Editor: Michele A. Petro

Design & Typography: Elizabeth M. Watson

Layout & Production: Patty Holden

Photography & Recipes: Teubner Foodfoto JmbH

Printed in China

ISBN: 1-59637-024-6

CONTENTS

SPRING ROLLS AND NOODLES

MEAT AND POULTRY

SEAFOOD

VEGETABLES

INTRODUCTION

FOR THOUSANDS OF YEARS, Chinese cooks have used woks to prepare delicious dishes in minutes. Because woks use less cooking oil than a frying pan, they are perfect for preparing wonderful, healthy meals.

BUYING A WOK

Look for a 14 to 16 inch wok, the heavier, the better. Your wok should have two handles; a long handle used to move and tilt the wok when cooking and a smaller handle on the opposite side to make it easy to lift the pan.

SHAPE

Many cooks choose a flat-bottom wok over traditional rounded-bottom woks. Flat-bottomed woks are more stable and are especially well-suited to stoves with electric burners.

MATERIAL

Carbon steel woks are relatively inexpensive and conduct heat evenly, making them a popular choice. Other choices include heavy gauge or hard anodized aluminum woks with a non-stick surface and more traditional cast iron woks. Although a non-stick aluminum wok will be easier to clean, it does not retain heat as well as carbon steel or iron woks, making it less effective in stir-frying. Cast iron does a better job of retaining heat than carbon steel, but the weight of a cast iron wok may make it difficult to handle. We recommend carbon steel for its relatively light weight, quick heat conduction, and excellent heat retention.

SEASONING YOUR WOK

Before you use your new carbon steel wok for the first time, you must prepare or "season" it. Note: if you choose an aluminum wok, do not attempt to season it—you will ruin the cooking surface.

To season a new carbon spun-steel wok, scrub it inside and out with hot soapy water and a scouring pad to remove the manufacturer's protective coating. Rinse it thoroughly and dry. Place the clean wok over high heat. Heat it until a few drops of water sprinkled into the wok immediately turn into dancing beads.

Dip a paper towel in peanut or canola oil and fold or wad the paper towel up into a ball. Use a pair of long-handled tongs or a spoon to then wipe the oil over the entire inside surface of the wok to coat it thoroughly. Reduce the heat to low and let the wok sit over the heat for 15 minutes to absorb the oil. Then remove the wok from the heat, let it cool completely, and wipe the oil off. In

time and with frequent use, the entire surface of your wok will turn black. Now your wok is properly seasoned!

CLEANING YOUR WOK

To clean your carbon steel wok, fill it with hot water and mild dish soap. Use a soft sponge or pad to gently clean off any food that is stuck to the wok. Never scrub your wok with an abrasive pad because this will remove the seasoning.

OTHER EQUIPMENT

You will need a sharp knife or cleaver to prepare your ingredients. In addition, have a spatula, wooden spoon, or a set of cooking chopsticks handy to stir the food as it cooks. Finally, be sure that you have a top or cover for your wok.

WOK STIR-FRY COOKING TECHNIQUES

Stir-frying is a fast cooking technique, requiring a series of quick, sequential steps in a very hot pan. Timing and rhythm are important, since interruptions or delays can cause you to over-cook your ingredients.

▶ Always use a cooking oil with a very high smoke point, such as peanut or canola oil.

▶ Heat the wok and then add 1 or 2 tablespoons of your cooking oil to the center of the wok. Spread the oil over the inside of the wok with a brush or by carefully tilting the wok to coat its sides.

▶ Prepare all your ingredients, including stock or other liquids, before you start cooking. Clean and chop your meat and vegetables ahead of time because you won't have time once you begin to cook.

▶ Cook your ingredients in small batches. Once you have added the food into the wok, stir and turn it with your cooking utensils (chop-sticks, spatula, or spoon) to spread it across the cooking surface. Remember, the pan is very hot so your ingredients will cook quickly. To slow the cooking process, push the food up the sides of the wok (the higher you go, the cooler the temperature of the pan) or move the food to a draining rack. Some woks come with internal racks for this purpose.

- ▶ Undercook everything. Remember, the ingredients will continue to cook even after you have removed them from the wok.
- ▶ Be careful when removing your food from the wok. The pan may be heavy and the food will be very hot, so be cautious. Loosen any food that may be stuck with your cooking utensil, grab the wok with both handles, and slide the food onto your dish or platter. Watch out for any grease or liquid splashes.

DON'T FORGET THE SPICES!

Spices and other flavoring are very important in stir-fry cooking. Since the flavors normally imparted by large quantities of fat are absent, you will want to add spices and other items to give your dishes an extra kick.

CHILE PEPPERS

Chile peppers are a favorite ingredient of stir-fry cooks and offer a wide range of flavors. Ranging from hot to very mild, chiles can add extra zing or subtle flavor to your food. Remember that the seeds and the ribs of a chile pepper are usually the hottest part. If you want just a hint of heat, add a whole chile pepper to your dish at the very end of the cooking process. Most of the dishes in this book call for serrano chiles. If you prefer less heat, use a jalapeño pepper. In general, the smaller the pepper, the spicier the flavor. Color is not an indication of spiciness.

CILANTRO

Cilantro adds a subtle Asian flavor to most dishes. You can substitute Italian parsley if you prefer something a bit mellower.

CLOUD EAR MUSHROOMS

A large form of the tree ear mushroom that is a delicately flavored, dried mushroom and resembles the bark of a tree. Reconstitute in water before using and trim off any tough portions before use.

GALANGAL

A relative of ginger that has a mustard-like flavor and is used in simmered dishes. It is sold in Asian markets in both fresh and dried forms: when using dried galangal, halve the quantity called for in a recipe and soak dried galangal in warm water until soft.

GINGER

Ginger adds a nice, zesty flavor to your dishes. Shop your local Asian markets for fresh ginger and store it for weeks in your refrigerator by peeling it and submerging in sherry.

KAFFIR LIME LEAVES

The leaves of a small, round uneven looking variety of lime native to Southeast Asia that add a strong citrus aroma and flavor to curries and simmered dishes. The leaves can be found fresh or frozen. You can also use 1½ teaspoons of finely grated lime zest for every two leaves called for in a recipe.

LEMON GRASS

Peel off the tough outer leaves. Intensify the lemon flavor by flattening the lemon grass stem before chopping. If lemon grass is unavailable, you can add a lemon flavor to your dish by substituting lemon peel.

MIRIN

A sweet rice wine used in Japanese cooking. Equal amounts of medium dry sherry may be substituted.

PALM SUGAR

A coarse, sticky, dark amber sugar made by boiling the sap of palm trees and sold in jars or cakes. If unavailable, substitute an equal amount of brown sugar.

TAMARIND PULP

Tamarind has a mild, fruity, sour taste. It is usually sold in eight ounce or one pound blocks. To use, break off a quarter-size piece and submerge in hot water. Wait about ten minutes until the tamarind has softened, rub the pulp with your fingers to extract all the flavor, then strain the liquid through a sieve. Discard pulp and use the liquid in your recipe.

The recipes in this book provide between two to four servings, depending on the number of other dishes served with the meal.

STEP-BY-STEP

1. Heat the wok then add the oil, spreading it all over the bottom and up the sides.

2. Begin adding the ingredients in small batches, starting with what will take the longest to cook.

3. Add more oil to the wok before adding other ingredients (e.g., meat, poultry, or seafood).

4. Continue adding additional ingredients.

5. Spread the ingredients across the cooking surface and up the sides to avoid over-cooking or remove them until later. Under-cook everything slightly since it will continue to cook once it's removed from the wok.

6. Continue to stir and toss ingredients with your cooking utensils.

7. Return everything to the wok and add spices and seasonings. Stir and toss until all ingredients are well seasoned.

8. Carefully remove everything from the wok and arrange on a platter or individual plates.

SPRING ROLLS AND NOODLES

NO BOOK ON WOK COOKING would be complete without recipes for crunchy wok-fried spring rolls and chewy stir-fried noodles. While homemade spring rolls may take a little extra effort, you can prepare them well in advance of your mealtime and freeze them for later use. The noodle dishes can be served either as a light entrée or as a side dish with more substantial entrées in the following chapters.

Spring Rolls with Vegetable Filling

Filling

2 medium carrots, peeled
1 large stalk celery
4 green onions
4 tbs peanut oil
1 clove garlic, minced
⅓ cup thinly shredded
    napa cabbage
⅓ cup shiitake mushrooms,
    tough stems discarded
    and thinly sliced
½ cup bean sprouts
½ cup snow peas
4 tbs soy sauce
1 tbs cornstarch
1 tbs finely
    chopped cilantro
Kosher salt
Freshly ground white pepper
Sweet and sour sauce or Chinese
    hot mustard for serving

1 tbs flour
8 spring roll wrappers
Vegetable oil for deep-frying

CUT CARROTS, CELERY, AND GREEN ONIONS into thin strips 2 inches long and ¼ inch wide.

IN A WOK, heat peanut oil and stir-fry garlic until it takes on a little color. Be careful not to burn garlic. Add vegetables one at a time and stir-fry for 2–3 minutes. Season with salt, pepper, and soy sauce. Stir cornstarch into a little cold water and use to thicken vegetables while stirring constantly. Add cilantro and mix well. Set aside vegetables and let cool.

WORK WITH ONE WRAPPER at a time and keep others covered with a damp towel. On a flat work surface, place 1–2 tablespoons of the vegetable mixture in the center of the wrapper. To seal the finished rolls, first, mix flour with 1 tablespoon cold water and then gradually stir in 2–3 tablespoons of hot water. Fold the bottom edge over the filling and spread the flour mixture onto the two side edges so they are sticky. Fold in the two side edges and brush the top end of the wrapper with the flour mixture. Lightly press all the edges together.

PLACE ROLLS IN 355°F oil in batches, fry until golden-brown, remove, and drain on paper towels.

SERVE IMMEDIATELY with a sweet and sour sauce or Chinese hot mustard.

Spring Rolls with a Spicy Dipping Sauce

Filling

1 medium carrot, peeled

1 large celery stalk

½ red bell pepper, seeds and stem removed and diced

2 small green onions, thinly sliced

2 tbs peanut oil

1 clove garlic, minced

½ tsp finely chopped lemon grass

1 tsp finely chopped ginger root

1 fresh small red serrano chile pepper

⅓ cup fresh bean sprouts, rinsed and drained well

1 tbs chopped cilantro

2–3 tbs light soy sauce

Kosher salt

Freshly ground pepper

12 spring roll wrappers (5 x 5 inch)

1 egg white, whisked (for sealing spring roll wrappers)

Vegetable oil for deep-frying

Dipping sauce

⅓ cup sweet and sour sauce

3 tbs chili and garlic sauce

1 tbs finely sliced green onions (green part only)

Lime juice to taste

Kosher salt

Freshly ground pepper

CUT CARROT AND CELERY into thin strips 2 inches long and ¼ inch wide.

IN A WOK OR PAN, heat peanut oil, add onions, garlic, lemon grass, ginger and chile pepper, and brown briefly. Add carrots, celery and bell peppers, and stir-fry for 3–4 minutes. Finally, add bean sprouts and fry for 1 minute. Season to taste with cilantro, soy sauce, salt, and pepper. Let cool.

WORK WITH ONE WRAPPER at a time and keep others covered with a damp towel. On a flat work surface, place a little filling in the center of the wrapper. Fold bottom edge far over the filling, fold in the right and left edges. Brush edges with egg white and roll up tightly. Press gently to seal and add more egg white, if necessary.

FOR THE DIPPING SAUCE: Combine sweet and sour and chili sauce in a bowl and stir until smooth. Stir in green onions and lime juice. If desired, season to taste with salt and pepper. Set aside.

IN A DEEP FRYER, heat oil to 355°F and fry rolls until golden-brown. Remove, drain well, and serve with dipping sauce.

Garden Vegetable Noodles

8 oz Chinese egg noodles (lo mein)
1 fresh red serrano chile pepper,
    remove stem and seeds
1 large carrot, peeled
¾ cup snow peas
½ large yellow bell pepper, remove
    stem and seeds
1 medium tomato, remove core
    and seeds
5 tbs peanut oil
1 clove garlic, finely chopped
Quarter-sized piece of fresh ginger
    root, finely chopped
2 green onions, cut into
    1 inch pieces
3 tbs light soy sauce
⅓ cup vegetable stock
1 fresh red serrano chile pepper,
    remove stem and seeds and
    cut into thin rings
2 large eggs
½ tbs peanut oil
Cucumber slices for garnish
Kosher salt
Freshly ground pepper

BRING A LARGE POT three-fourths full of water to a boil. Add the noodles, stir to loosen the strands, return to a boil, and cook until tender, about 1–2 minutes. Drain, rinse thoroughly with cold running water, and drain again.

CUT CHILE PEPPER into thin rings. Cut carrot into thin strips 2 inches long and ¼ inch wide. Trim ends of snow peas and cut diagonally into ½ inch pieces. Cut bell pepper into thin strips 2 inches long and ¼ inch wide. Cut tomato into ¼ inch dice.

IN A WOK, heat peanut oil until smoking hot. Fry noodles until crispy, remove, and set aside. Add garlic, ginger and chile pepper, and brown briefly. Add carrots, snow peas, bell peppers and green onions, and stir-fry for 3–4 minutes. Add tomatoes and fry for 1 minute. Remove vegetables from wok. Season with soy sauce, vegetable stock, salt, and pepper; add fried noodles and fry briefly.

HEAT HALF TABLESPOON OF PEANUT OIL, if needed. Beat eggs with salt. Add chile peppers to hot oil and cook briefly. Add egg mixture and scramble. Return vegetables and noodles to wok and gently fold in egg mixture.

PLACE IN SERVING DISH and garnish with cucumber slices, if desired.

Rainbow Salad

1 medium cucumber
2 carrots, peeled
1 large red bell pepper
1 large yellow bell pepper, stem
    and seeds removed
3 green onions
¾ cup bean sprouts
4 tbs peanut oil, separated
½ cup fresh shiitake mushrooms,
    stems removed and sliced
2 eggs
Kosher salt

Sauce

3 tbs sesame paste (Tahini)
2–3 tbs water
1 tbs rice vinegar
Kosher salt
Freshly ground pepper

CUT CUCUMBER in half lengthwise, scrape out seeds with a small spoon, and slice thinly. Sprinkle slices with a little salt and let stand for 10 minutes. Slice carrots thin diagonally. Cut bell peppers into ½ inch cubes. Cut green onions into pieces 1½ inches long. Sort bean sprouts.

FOR THE SAUCE: Combine sesame paste and water in a bowl and stir until smooth. Stir in vinegar and season to taste with salt and pepper.

IN A WOK, heat 3 tablespoons peanut oil, add carrots and bell peppers, and stir-fry for 1 minute. Add green onions and shiitakes and stir-fry for 1 minute. Add bean sprouts and stir-fry for 1 minute. Remove vegetables, let cool, and fold in well-drained cucumbers.

IN A BOWL, whisk eggs with a fork and season lightly with salt and pepper. In a pan, heat ½ tablespoon peanut oil. Add half the eggs and tilt pan to cover the bottom. Fry until light-brown, turn, and fry the other side. Remove and let cool. In the same way, make the second omelet. Cut omelets in half and then into strips about 1½ inches wide.

POUR SAUCE over vegetables and mix carefully. Transfer to plates and garnish with omelet strips.

Crispy Noodles

2 green onions
1 fresh red serrano chile pepper,
    stems, ribs, and seeds removed
8 oz Chinese egg noodles (lo mein)
2–3 tbs peanut oil
1 tbs oyster sauce
3 tbs light soy sauce
1 tsp galangal root, peeled and
    finely diced
2 cloves garlic, finely diced
Kosher salt
Freshly ground pepper

CUT GREEN ONIONS and chile pepper into fine strips.

COOK NOODLES in a large pot of boiling, salted water for 1–2 minutes and drain well.

IN A WOK, heat peanut oil until smoking hot. Fry noodles until crispy, season to taste with oyster sauce and light soy sauce, remove from the wok, and set aside.

ADD GREEN ONIONS, galangal root, garlic, and chile pepper to the wok and stir-fry. Return noodles to the wok and stir well. If desired, season to taste with salt and pepper.

Peppery
Egg Noodles
with Shrimp

14 oz Chinese egg noodles
1 fresh green serrano chile pepper,
    stem removed
1 small red bell pepper, stem,
    seeds, and ribs removed
1 small yellow bell pepper, stem,
    seeds, and ribs removed
⅓ lb oyster mushrooms, cleaned
⅓ cup canned bamboo
    shoots, drained
4 tbs peanut oil
8 raw peeled and deveined shrimp
Quarter-sized piece of fresh ginger
    root, diced
1 clove garlic, diced
2 green onions, sliced
3 tbs light soy sauce
Cilantro for garnish
Kosher salt
Freshly ground pepper

COOK NOODLES in boiling, salted water for 1–2 minutes, pour into a colander, rinse under cold water, and set aside.

CUT CHILE PEPPER crosswise into rings. Cut bell peppers, oyster mushrooms, and bamboo shoots into strips.

IN A WOK, heat peanut oil, fry shrimp for 2 minutes, and remove. Add ginger, chile pepper and bell peppers to the wok, and fry for 2 minutes, then add garlic and stir fry for another minute. Add oyster mushrooms, green onions and bamboo shoots, and fry for another 2–3 minutes. Add noodles and shrimp and fry for another 2–3 minutes. Season to taste with salt, pepper, and soy sauce.

SPRINKLE with cilantro and serve.

Sesame Chinese Noodles with Tofu and Mushrooms

1 small red bell pepper, seeds,
    stem, and ribs removed
¼ lb shiitake mushrooms,
    cleaned and stems removed
2 green onions
2 fresh serrano chile peppers,
    seeds and stems removed
8 oz Chinese wheat noodles
2 tbs sesame oil
8 oz firm tofu, drained and dried
⅓ cup celery, finely diced
3 tbs light soy sauce
2 tbs sesame oil
Toasted sesame seeds for garnish
Kosher salt
Freshly ground pepper

CUT BELL PEPPER into ¾ inch cubes. Cut shiitake mushroom caps into quarters. Chop green onions into rings. Cut tofu into ¾ inch cubes. Cut chile peppers into thin strips.

COOK NOODLES in boiling, salted water until al dente and set aside.

IN A WOK OR PAN, heat sesame oil and brown tofu, then remove. Add bell pepper, shiitakes, celery, green onions and chile peppers, and brown in the wok. Add noodles. Add soy sauce and stir well. Add salt and pepper, if desired. Add tofu, stir in sesame oil, and serve.

GARNISH noodles with toasted sesame seeds.

Wide Noodles with Tofu and Shrimp

6 oz wide egg noodles
1 green onion
1 cup baby corn
⅓ lb squash flesh (acorn
    or butternut)
7 oz firm tofu
4 tbs peanut oil
8 raw medium shrimp,
    peeled and deveined
1 clove garlic, peeled and
    finely chopped
2 tsp fresh galangal, peeled
    and finely chopped
1 small red serrano chile
    pepper, stem, seeds, and
    ribs removed and chopped
1 cup snow peas, cleaned
1 tbs chopped cilantro
Kosher salt
Freshly ground pepper

Seasoning sauce
½ cup vegetable stock
2 tbs soy sauce
2 tbs oyster sauce
½ tsp cornstarch

COOK EGG NOODLES in boiling, salted water just until al dente, drain, rinse under cold water, and set aside until needed.

CUT GREEN ONIONS into pieces 1 inch long. Blanch baby corn in boiling, salted water for 2 minutes, plunge into cold water, drain well, and cut in half crosswise. Cut squash into ½ inch cubes and tofu into ¾ inch cubes.

FOR THE SEASONING SAUCE: Combine stock, soy sauce, oyster sauce and cornstarch in a small bowl, and stir well.

IN A WOK, heat peanut oil, stir-fry tofu for 3–4 minutes and remove. Add shrimp to wok, fry for 1–2 minutes, and remove. Add green onions, garlic, galangal root and chile pepper, and stir-fry. Add baby corn, snow peas and squash, and stir-fry for 5–6 minutes until crunchy. Pour in seasoning sauce and bring to a boil. Carefully stir in tofu, shrimp and egg noodles, and heat briefly. Season with salt, pepper and cilantro, and serve.

Malaysian Tomato-Chile Noodles

1⅓ lb tomatoes
1 tbs peanut oil
2 fresh green serrano chile
   peppers, stems, seeds and
   ribs removed, and diced
1 small onion, peeled and
   finely diced
3 cloves garlic, minced
3 fresh lime leaves, thinly sliced
   (or 1 tsp dried)
1 tsp palm or brown sugar
8 oz Malaysian longevity or
   Shanghai style noodles
Lime wedges for garnish
Kosher salt

REMOVE TOMATO LEAVES and set aside. Place tomatoes briefly in boiling water, plunge into cold water, peel, cut into quarters, remove cores and seeds, and dice finely.

IN A WOK OR PAN, heat peanut oil, chile peppers and onions, and stir-fry for 4 minutes. Add garlic and stir fry for another minute until fragrant. Add lime leaves, season with sugar and salt, and simmer over moderate heat for 20–25 minutes.

IN THE MEANTIME, boil noodles in boiling, salted water until al dente and drain well. Mix noodles with sauce, transfer to plates or a serving dish, and serve. Garnish with lime wedges.

TIP

▶ If unable to find Malaysian or Shanghai noodles, Chinese egg noodles can be used. Boil egg noodles for 1–2 minutes in boiling, salted water and drain well. Mix with sauce and serve.

MEAT AND POULTRY

COOKING MEAT OR POULTRY IN YOUR WOK is perfect for today's busy lifestyle. Quick searing of meat in a fiery hot wok adds a dimension of flavor unmatched in any other style of cooking, and the high heat helps to concentrate the flavors of your sauce or marinade while caramelizing the natural sugars in your food. Braising less tender cuts of meat in a wok is also an excellent way to enhance the flavor in your finished dish.

Flank Steak with Crunchy Noodles

1 lb flank steak, trimmed
2 green onions
½ each yellow and green bell
    peppers, seeds, stems, and
    ribs removed
4 tbs peanut oil
1 tsp crushed Szechwan peppercorns
1 star anise
2 tbs minced fresh ginger root
1 clove garlic, chopped
¾ cup beef stock
½ lb tomatoes, cores and seeds
    removed, and quartered
2 tbs light soy sauce
1 tsp palm sugar or light
    brown sugar
½ tsp cornstarch
7 oz rice vermicelli noodles
1 tbs chopped Chinese chives
Vegetable oil for deep-frying
Kosher salt
Freshly ground pepper

REMOVE FAT from the meat and slice thinly against the grain. Cut green onions into pieces about ¾ inch long. Cut bell peppers into ½ inch diamonds.

IN A WOK, heat peanut oil, fry Szechwan pepper for 1–2 minutes until it gives off a fragrance, and remove. Fry meat in the wok in batches for 2–3 minutes. Add star anise, green onions, bell peppers, ginger and garlic, and fry for 1–2 minutes. Pour in beef stock and add tomatoes and pepper. Season to taste with soy sauce, sugar and salt, and braise for 4–5 minutes. Stir cornstarch into a little cold water to dissolve, add to wok, bring to a boil, and add seasoning to taste.

PICK APART raw rice noodles. In a separate large skillet, deep-fry noodles in oil until they swell. Remove and briefly drain on paper towels. Arrange noodles on serving platter and top with flank steak. Serve sprinkled with Chinese chives.

Sliced Beef Tenderloin with Vegetables

¾ lb beef tenderloin

Marinade
½ cup dark soy sauce
2 tsp Chinese
    five-spice powder
2 pinches ground coriander
2 pinches ground cumin
Kosher salt
Freshly ground pepper

Vinaigrette
⅓ cup plus 2 tbs beef stock
1 clove garlic, chopped
½ tsp freshly grated ginger
2 pinches Chinese
    five-spice powder
2 tbs plus 1½ tsp light
    soy sauce
¼ cup toasted sesame oil
2 tbs vegetable oil
2 tbs Chinese vinegar

Rice
13 oz medium grain Japanese rice
Salt
¼ cup sesame oil, separated
4 tbs beef stock

Vegetables
½ small yellow, green, and red
    bell peppers (½ of each)
½ cup snow peas, cleaned
¼ lb shiitake mushrooms, stems
    removed and sliced
⅓ cup bean sprouts

TRIM BEEF thoroughly, slice thinly, and place in a bowl.

FOR THE MARINADE: Combine all the ingredients listed and pour over the meat. Cover and marinate in the refrigerator for 2 hours.

FOR THE VINAIGRETTE: Pour stock into a saucepan, add garlic, ginger and five-spice powder, and reduce by half over medium heat. Transfer to a bowl and stir in soy sauce, oils, and vinegar.

PREHEAT OVEN TO 425°F. Bake bell peppers until the peel blisters, remove, and let "sweat" in a plastic bag. Peel and cut into fine strips. Cut snow peas crosswise into strips.

RINSE RICE under cold running water. Place rice in covered saucepan and add water until it rises an inch above the rice. Bring to a boil, cover, and simmer on low heat for 15–20 minutes, until water is absorbed.

IN A WOK, heat 2 tablespoons of sesame oil until smoking hot and stir-fry meat slices. Remove.

HEAT REMAINING sesame oil in the wok and brown bell pepper strips. Add snow peas and mushrooms and fry for 2–3 minutes. Add bean sprouts and stir-fry briefly. Pour in vinaigrette. Return meat to the wok and stir. Add beef stock and stir.

Pork with
Crisp Vegetables

¾ lb pork tenderloin
1 red bell pepper, stems, seeds,
    and ribs removed
1 yellow bell pepper, stems, seeds,
    and ribs removed
½ lb broccoli
1 bunch green onions
3 tbs peanut oil
2 cloves garlic, minced
Soy sauce (optional)
2 sprigs Italian parsley for garnish
Kosher salt
Freshly ground white pepper

CUT MEAT into small, thin slices. Cut bell peppers into strips. Rinse broccoli, divide into small florets, peel stems, and slice finely. Chop green onions into thin rings.

IN A WOK, heat 1½ tablespoons peanut oil until smoking hot. Add meat and garlic and fry briefly while turning 2–3 times. Remove immediately and transfer to a plate.

IN REMAINING PEANUT OIL, fry bell peppers and ginger for about 3–4 minutes, then add broccoli and green onions, and fry for 3–5 minutes. The vegetables should remain crisp. Add meat to the vegetables. Season with salt, pepper, and soy sauce, if desired.

GARNISH with parsley sprigs and serve with rice.

Pork with Cream and Mushrooms

6 dried cloud ear mushrooms

2 pork cutlets (about ¾ lb each)

1 green bell pepper, stem, seeds, and ribs removed

1 onion

3 tbs vegetable oil

¾ cup heavy cream

1 jar sliced mushrooms (about ½ cup), drained

1 tbs light soy sauce

2 tbs chopped Italian parsley

SOAK MUSHROOMS in cold water for about 10 minutes, remove from water, and chop coarsely.

CUT PORK into thin strips. Cut bell pepper into fine strips. Cut onion into rings.

IN A WOK, heat 1 tablespoon vegetable oil until smoking hot. Stir-fry meat for 1 minute and remove from pan. Add onions and bell peppers and stir-fry for 2–3 minutes. Remove from pan and pour out any remaining oil. Pour cream into the wok and bring to a boil. Add meat and vegetables and season generously to taste with soy sauce. Stir in parsley and serve with rice.

Thai Pork Stir-Fry

½ lb trimmed pork tenderloin
1 clove garlic, minced
1 fresh red chile pepper, minced
1 inch piece lemon grass, minced
1 tbs fresh ginger root, peeled
    and minced
2 tbs Asian chili sauce
1½ tbs light soy sauce
1½ tbs fish sauce
6 tbs sesame oil, separated
2 tbs rice wine
½ tsp mild curry powder
2 tsp cilantro, minced
1–2 green onions
⅓ cup green asparagus
A little cornstarch
3 tbs peanut oil
¼ cup shiitake mushrooms, tough
    stems removed and sliced
¼ cup red bell pepper, diced
¼ cup yellow bell pepper, diced
¼ cup snow peas, cleaned and
    thinly sliced
⅓ cup bean sprouts, sort, rinse,
    and drain
½ cup chicken stock
Cilantro for garnish
Kosher salt
Freshly ground pepper

CUT PORK across the grain into fine slices and place in a bowl. Add garlic, chile pepper, lemon grass and ginger to chili sauce, soy sauce, fish sauce, 4 tablespoons sesame oil, rice wine, curry powder, pepper, and cilantro with the meat. Cover and marinate for 30 minutes.

CHOP GREEN ONIONS into fine rings. Cut asparagus into pieces 1½ inches long.

REMOVE MEAT from marinade. Bring marinade to a boil and simmer for 5 minutes. Set aside.

DUST PORK with a little cornstarch. In a wok, heat peanut oil, stir-fry meat for about 2 minutes and remove. Briefly brown green onions and shiitakes. Add remaining vegetables, drizzle on remaining sesame oil, and stir-fry for 3–4 minutes. Pour in marinade and stock, return meat to the wok, and simmer for 1 minute. Season to taste with salt and pepper. Sprinkle with cilantro and serve.

TIP

▶ Stir-fried pork tenderloin slices and vegetables are ready in a flash.
▶ If you make this dish for more than one person, be sure to fry the meat in batches so the temperature of the oil remains high enough to brown it quickly.

Chicken Breast in a Honey Ginger Marinade

Marinade

1 tbs honey

½ tsp ginger

3 tbs vinegar

1 tsp chili oil

2 tbs vegetable oil

1 tsp grated peel from
   an organic orange

¼ cup plum wine

Kosher salt

1 lb boneless, skinless chicken
   breast fillets

1 large celery stalk, cleaned
   and rinsed

3 green onions

1 fresh green chile pepper (jalapeño
   or serrano), seeds removed

⅓ lb fresh diced mango, peeled

3 tbs vegetable oil

¼ lb cherry tomatoes,
   cores removed

½ cup canned lychees

1 tbs chopped parsley

COMBINE ALL the ingredients together for the marinade and mix.

RINSE CHICKEN BREAST fillets, pat dry with paper towels, and cut into fine strips. Add to marinade and marinate for 1 hour.

IN THE MEANTIME, Cut celery into fine matchsticks. Chop green onions and chile pepper into rings. Cut mango into cubes of about ½ inch.

REMOVE MEAT from marinade, drain, and save marinade. Bring marinade to a boil and simmer for 5 minutes. Set aside.

IN A WOK, heat vegetable oil until very hot. Add meat and brown quickly and then place on a draining rack. Add celery to the wok and cook for about 1 minute. Add tomatoes, onions and chile pepper, and braise briefly. Stir in lychees and mango and then meat. Heat and add reserved marinade. Sprinkle with parsley and serve immediately with rice.

Braised Chicken with Vegetables and Egg Noodles

1½ lb skinless, boneless
    chicken thighs
5 tbs peanut oil
3–4 green onions
1 fresh red chile pepper, stems,
    seeds, and ribs removed
½ large red bell pepper, stems,
    seeds, and ribs removed
½ lb green asparagus
1 clove garlic, diced
1½ tsp fresh ginger, peeled
    and diced
1 small carrot, peeled and sliced
⅓–½ cup chicken stock
4 tbs soy sauce
1 tbs dark soy sauce
5 oz lo mein noodles
5–6 cloud ear mushrooms, soaked,
    drained, and chopped
1 tbs finely chopped cilantro
Kosher salt
Freshly ground pepper

RINSE CHICKEN under cold running water and drain well. Cut each thigh into 3–4 pieces. Season with salt and pepper.

IN A WOK, heat peanut oil over medium high heat and brown meat on all sides. Reduce heat and fry for 5–10 minutes until no longer pink.

CHOP GREEN ONIONS into fine rings. Cut chile pepper into fine strips. Cut bell pepper into ½ inch slices. Remove bottom ends from asparagus, peeling bottom third if necessary, and cut into pieces 1½ inches long.

REMOVE MEAT from wok and keep warm. Remove all but 2 tablespoons oil from the wok. Add green onions, chile pepper, garlic and ginger, and brown briefly. Add bell peppers, carrots and asparagus, and stir-fry for 8–10 minutes. Add chicken stock, soy sauce, salt and pepper, and stir in meat.

COOK NOODLES in a large pot of boiling, salted water until al dente about 1–2 minutes and drain well. Stir noodles, mushrooms, and cilantro into the vegetable-meat mixture, add seasoning to taste and serve.

Golden

Chicken Curry

1½ lb boneless, skinless
    chicken thigh
¾ lb small new potatoes, peeled
2 large carrots, peeled
4 cups coconut milk
1 large onion, coarsely chopped
1 tbs vegetable oil
½ tsp salt
2 tbs sugar
4 tbs fish sauce

Curry paste
12 dried red chile peppers
1 large shallot, peeled and
    coarsely chopped
1 tbs coriander root, cleaned
    and chopped
1 tbs lemon grass, cleaned
    and chopped
1 tbs ground cumin
5 tsp ground turmeric

1 cup basmati rice
Cilantro for garnish
Kosher salt
Freshly ground pepper

RINSE CHICKEN under cold running water, pat dry, and cut into 1 inch cubes. Cover and refrigerate until ready to use.

FOR THE CURRY PASTE: Soak dried chile peppers in cold water for 20 minutes, and then thoroughly drain. In a blender or food processor, combine chile peppers, shallots, coriander root and lemon grass, and process into a smooth paste. Stir in cumin and turmeric.

CUT POTATOES into ¾ inch cubes. Cut carrots into ½ inch diagonal pieces.

IN A WOK, bring coconut milk to a boil over medium heat, add chicken, and simmer for 10 minutes. Add potatoes, carrots, and onions.

IN A SAUCEPAN, heat oil. Add ⅔ cup coconut milk from the wok. Stir in curry paste and simmer for 10 minutes. Pour mixture into the wok and season with salt, sugar, and fish sauce. Simmer over low heat for another 15–20 minutes and add seasoning to taste.

IN THE MEANTIME, rinse rice under cold water, place in a bowl, cover with cold water, and soak for 20–30 minutes. Drain and transfer to a saucepan. Add 2 cups water and a dash of salt. Bring to a boil, reduce heat, and cook for 12–15 minutes until most of the liquid has been absorbed. Transfer rice and chicken curry to preheated plates and serve garnished with cilantro.

Asian Style

Fried Chicken

1 lb boneless, skinless chicken
    breast fillets
1 medium yellow bell pepper, stem
    and seeds removed, and sliced

Marinade
2 tbs dark soy sauce
2 tbs sake (rice wine)
1 tsp freshly grated ginger root

Batter coating
2 egg whites
3 tbs cornstarch
¼ tsp salt
½ tsp turmeric
3–4 green onions (a little green
    part), cleaned and chopped
1 tbs chopped fresh ginger root
Cornstarch for breading
Vegetable oil for deep-frying
Soy sauce with chili pepper
    flakes for serving
Kosher salt

CUT CHICKEN into pieces 1½ inches long and ½ inch wide.

FOR THE MARINADE: Combine all the ingredients listed. Place chicken pieces in a shallow dish, pour marinade evenly over the top, cover, and refrigerate for 30 minutes.

FOR THE BATTER COATING: Beat egg whites until foamy and fold in cornstarch. Fold in salt, turmeric, green onions, and ginger. Remove chicken from marinade and drain. Dredge in cornstarch, knocking off excess, then dip in egg white mixture.

IN A WOK, heat oil over medium high heat and deep-fry chicken until crispy. Remove and drain. Deep-fry bell pepper strips until tender on the outside (don't cook longer than 30 seconds), remove, drain, and season with salt. Arrange chicken and bell peppers on serving dish. Serve soy sauce with chili pepper flakes on the side.

Bami Goreng

Pancake batter

⅓ cup flour
1 egg
1 egg yolk
⅓ cup plus 2 tbs milk
1 tbs butter for frying

1½ lb boneless, skinless
    chicken breasts
4–5 green onions, cleaned
2 small fresh serrano red chile
    peppers, stems and
    seeds removed
8 medium raw shrimp, peeled
    and deveined
10 oz thin Asian egg noodles
½ cup peanut oil
1 small onion, minced
3 cloves garlic, minced
⅓ lb bok choy, rinsed and sliced
1 tbs diced fresh galangal root
1 tsp sugar
2 tbs light soy sauce
¼ cup chicken stock
1 tsp chopped cilantro
Kosher salt

FOR THE PANCAKE BATTER: Sift flour into a bowl and stir in egg, egg yolk, pinch of salt, and milk to form a smooth batter. Cover and let stand for 20 minutes.

CUT CHICKEN into about ¾ inch cubes. Cut green onions into 1 inch pieces. Cut chiles into thin strips. Leave on the last segment of the shrimp tail.

COOK THE NOODLES in boiling, salted water for 1–2 minutes, rinse under cold water, and drain well.

FOR THE PANCAKES: Melt a little butter in a pan, pour in some batter, spread out evenly, and fry on both sides until golden. Repeat the same procedure until all the batter has been used. Cut pancakes into thin strips.

IN A WOK, heat peanut oil until smoking hot. Brown noodles until crispy, remove, and set aside. Add chicken to wok and brown on all sides. Add green onions, onions and garlic, and stir-fry. Stir in bok choy and fry. Add chile peppers, galangal root and shrimp, and fry about 1–2 minutes. Season with salt, sugar, soy sauce, and chicken stock. Add fried noodles and fry briefly. Stir in cilantro.

SERVE BAMI GORENG garnished with pancake strips.

Sweet Chili Chicken

1½ lb boneless, skinless chicken
    breast fillets
4 green onions
⅓ lb green beans
1 small green bell pepper, seeds,
    stem, and ribs removed
⅔ cup snow peas
1 large celery stalk
¾ cup chicken stock
2 tbs sweet chili sauce
2 tbs light soy sauce
¼ tsp cornstarch
3 tbs peanut oil
1 inch piece fresh ginger
    root, minced
2 cloves garlic, minced
⅓ cup frozen peas
1 fresh red serrano chile pepper,
    seeds and stems removed,
    and diced
1 tbs finely chopped cilantro
Cilantro for garnish
Kosher salt
Freshly ground pepper

CUT CHICKEN into ¾ inch cubes. Cut green onions diagonally into pieces about 1 inch long. Trim ends from beans and cut into pieces about 1 inch long. Cut bell pepper into thin strips. Trim ends from snow peas and leave whole or cut in half crosswise, depending on the size. Remove any tough thick threads from celery with a vegetable peeler.

IN A BOWL, combine chicken stock, chili sauce, soy sauce, salt, pepper and cornstarch, and mix well.

IN A WOK, heat peanut oil and sear meat for 2 minutes. Add ginger and garlic; reduce heat and fry for another 2 minutes. Add green onions, beans, bell peppers, celery, and chicken stock mixture, cover and simmer for another 2–3 minutes. Add snow peas, peas and chile pepper, and fry for another 2–3 minutes. Add seasoning to taste and toss with chopped cilantro. Transfer to serving dish and garnish with cilantro.

Spicy Cashew Chicken

1½ lb boneless, skinless chicken
    breast fillets
1 small onion
2 green onions
1 large red bell pepper, stem,
    seeds, and ribs removed
1 fresh red serrano chile pepper,
    stems removed
3 tbs peanut oil
¼ cup cashews
2 cloves garlic, minced
½ tbs red curry paste
1 tbs oyster sauce
2 tbs light soy sauce
1 tbs fish sauce
1 pinch brown sugar
½ cup chicken stock
¼ tsp cornstarch
1 tbs toasted sesame seeds
Several cilantro leaves for garnish
Kosher salt

CUT CHICKEN into strips. Cut onion in half and then into strips. Cut green onions into pieces about 1½ inches long. Cut bell peppers into cubes of about ½ inch. Cut chile pepper into rings.

IN A WOK, heat peanut oil, stir-fry cashews until golden-brown, remove, and set aside. Add garlic, chile pepper and chicken to wok, and stir-fry for 1–2 minutes. Stir in curry paste and roast briefly. Add onion strips, bell peppers and green onions, and stir-fry for 1–2 minutes. Add oyster sauce, soy sauce, fish sauce, sugar, and stock. Check seasoning. Stir cornstarch into a little water, use to thicken sauce, and bring to a boil.

SPRINKLE with reserved cashews and sesame seeds and garnish with cilantro.

Fragrant Chicken and Green Onions

1¾ lb boneless, skinless chicken
    breast fillets
3 green onions
1 clove garlic, minced
1½ tbs diced fresh ginger root
1 fresh red chile pepper,
    stem removed
2 tbs peanut oil
⅓ lb shiitake mushrooms, stems
    removed and sliced
¼ cup light soy sauce
1 cup chicken stock
1 tsp cornstarch
2 tbs chopped mint leaves
Kosher salt
Freshly ground pepper

CUT CHICKEN BREAST FILLETS into strips. Cut green onions into pieces about 1½ inches long. Cut chile pepper into fine rings.

IN A WOK, heat peanut oil, add chicken, season with salt and pepper, and brown. Add green onions, shiitakes, garlic, chile pepper and ginger, and fry for 2 minutes. Pour in soy sauce and stock. Add seasoning to taste. Stir cornstarch into a little water and use to thicken sauce. Add mint. Serve with rice.

Coconut Curry Turkey Cutlets

½ cup rice
½ lb turkey breast cutlets
2 green onions
1 tbs canned coconut
    milk, unsweetened
1 tbs lemon juice
2 tsp curry
1 tbs sugar
1 tbs canola or peanut oil
½ mango, diced
Kosher salt
Freshly ground pepper

COOK RICE in 1 cup salted water brought to a boil. Cover tightly, then simmer for 20 minutes over low heat.

CUT TURKEY BREAST into small pieces and season with salt and pepper. Cut green onions diagonally into pieces.

COMBINE COCONUT CREAM, lemon juice, 2 tablespoons water, curry, and sugar.

SEAR TURKEY in oil for 2 minutes on each side, remove from pan, and set aside. Add onions and mango and braise over medium heat for 5 minutes. Pour in curry sauce, add turkey cutlets, and simmer for 1 minute. Arrange rice and curry sauce on a plate. Garnish with diced mango from sauce.

Duck with Butternut Squash

4 duck breasts (about 8 oz each)

¼ lb butternut squash, peeled and
    seeds removed

½ small red bell pepper, stem,
    seeds, and ribs removed

1 stalk celery

1 cup snow peas

2 green onions

2 fresh red chile peppers (jalapeño
    or serrano)

3 tbs vegetable oil

1 clove garlic, peeled and chopped

½ tsp freshly grated ginger

2 tbs light soy sauce

1 tbs rice wine

1 tsp sugar

¼ cup chicken stock

1 tbs diced celery leaves

½ tsp salt

1 tbs rice vinegar

½ tsp coarsely crushed
    Szechwan peppercorns

½ tsp cornstarch

RINSE DUCK BREASTS and pat dry. Remove skin and cut meat into strips ½ inch wide.

CUT SQUASH into slices ⅛ inch thick and then into thin matchsticks. Cut bell peppers into cubes of about ⅓ inch. Cut celery into fine strips about 2 inches long. Remove stems from snow peas and cut in half diagonally. Cut green onions diagonally into rings.

IN A WOK, heat vegetable oil on medium-high heat and sear duck meat in batches. Remove with a slotted spoon and keep warm.

IN THE REMAINING OIL, briefly brown chile peppers and green onions, stirring several times. Add squash and fry for 1 minute. Add bell peppers, celery and snow peas one at a time, and stir-fry with 1 minute intervals in between each item.

ADD GARLIC, ginger, soy sauce, rice wine, sugar, chicken stock, celery leaves, salt, rice vinegar, and Szechwan pepper. Stir cornstarch into a little water and use to thicken vegetable mixture.

ADD FRIED, SEARED DUCK MEAT and simmer for 2 minutes until the sauce has thickened. Season to taste and serve.

TIP

▶ Szechwan peppercorns are available in Asian markets and give many dishes their unmistakable flavor.

▶ In China, this poultry dish is usually prepared with butternut squash, which has dark-yellow flesh that gives off a pleasant fragrance from which it takes its name. For this recipe, any local variety of butternut squash can be used.

Sizzling Chile Duck Breast

2 duck breasts (about 7 oz each)
1 small onion
2 fresh green serrano chile peppers,
   stems removed
1 small red bell pepper, stem,
   seeds, and ribs removed
½ cup snow peas
1 clove garlic, minced
1½ tsp minced fresh ginger root
½ cup carrot, peeled and
   thinly sliced
4 tbs peanut or vegetable oil
Cooked basmati rice

Sauce
4 tbs light soy sauce
1 tbs sweet soy sauce
2 tbs rice wine
1 cup duck or chicken stock
1 tsp cornstarch
Kosher salt
Freshly ground pepper

CUT DUCK BREAST into thin slices. Cut onion into thin rings. Cut chile peppers crosswise into fine rings. Cut bell pepper into fine strips. Trim ends from snow peas, and then cut into ¾ inch diagonal slices.

THOROUGHLY MIX all sauce ingredients together and set aside.

IN A WOK, heat oil, season duck with salt and pepper, and stir-fry in batches, removing after 2–3 minutes. Add onions, garlic, ginger and chile peppers to the wok, and fry for 1 minute. Add bell peppers, carrots and snow peas, and stir-fry for 3–4 minutes. Return duck to the wok, pour in sauce, and bring to a boil. Add seasoning to taste and serve with basmati rice.

TIP

▶ If sauce is not thick enough, mix ¼ teaspoon cornstarch in 1 teaspoon cold water and add to sauce. Bring just to a boil.
▶ Duck is especially suitable for cooking in a wok because of its excellent meat-to-fat ratio. When stir-fried at a high temperature, the meat's full aroma develops without drying out.

SEAFOOD

COOKING SEAFOOD IN A WOK requires careful timing. A blistering hot wok can seal in the natural goodness in seafood without toughing the exterior, if properly monitored. To guard against overcooking: cut your seafood into uniform, small pieces, have all of other ingredients measured and ready before you start cooking, and carefully watch your seafood while it cooks.

Shrimp in a Spicy Coconut Sauce

24 large raw shrimp, peeled
    and deveined
2 tbs vegetable oil
Cilantro for garnish

Marinade
1 tbs tamarind pulp
1 clove garlic, minced
1 tbs minced fresh ginger
    root, minced
2 fresh small red chile peppers
    (jalapeño or serrano), stems,
    seeds and ribs removed,
    and diced
½ tsp turmeric
1 tsp salt

Coconut sauce
2 cloves garlic, crushed
¼ cup canned coconut milk
1 tbs chopped cilantro
2 fresh small green chile peppers
    (jalapeño or serrano), stems,
    seeds and ribs removed,
    and diced
Kosher salt

LEAVE LAST SEGMENT of the tail on the shrimp and place shrimp in a dish.

FOR THE MARINADE: Add ⅓ cup water with tamarind pulp and put pulp through a strainer and reserve liquid. Combine garlic, ginger, tamarind liquid, chile peppers, turmeric, and salt. Distribute marinade evenly over the shrimp, cover, and refrigerate for about 10 minutes.

REMOVE SHRIMP from marinade and drain well.

IN A WOK or large pan, heat vegetable oil and fry shrimp on both sides for 1–2 minutes, remove, and set aside. Prepare coconut sauce by adding crushed garlic to the wok and fry until light-brown. Add coconut milk, cilantro and chile peppers, and simmer for 5 minutes. Season to taste with salt.

TRANSFER SHRIMP to serving plate, top with sauce from the wok or pan, and garnish with cilantro.

Wild Salmon with Rice and English Peas

8 oz wild salmon fillet, skinned
Juice from ½ lime
1 tsp finely chopped dill
1 slice smoked bacon, diced
2 tbs sunflower oil or canola oil
1 cup long-grain rice
1 pinch saffron
1¼ cups chicken stock
¾ cup frozen green English peas
Kosher salt
Freshly ground pepper

CUT SALMON into cubes of about ½ inch. Season with salt, pepper, lime juice and dill, and refrigerate.

IN A WOK, heat oil and briefly stir-fry bacon. Add rice and stir briefly. Add stock. Stir in saffron, salt and pepper, and bring to a boil. Reduce heat, cover, and simmer for 20 minutes. For the last 5 minutes, add and simmer salmon and peas. Add seasoning to taste and serve.

Vegetable and Shrimp with Chinese Noodles

½ lb Chinese egg noodles

1–2 green onions

⅓ cup canned or fresh baby corn

⅓ lb squash (acorn, butternut, or pumpkin), peeled and seeds removed

¼ cup canned bamboo shoots

3 tbs peanut oil

8 raw shrimp, peeled and deveined

1 clove garlic, minced

1 fresh red serrano chile pepper, stem removed and diced

⅔ cup snow peas, ends removed

½ cup vegetable stock

⅓ lb cherry tomatoes, cores removed and halved

4 tbs soy sauce

1 tbs oyster sauce

1 tbs chopped cilantro for garnish

Kosher salt

Freshly ground pepper

COOK NOODLES in boiling, salted water until al dente and drain.

CUT GREEN ONIONS into pieces about ¾ inches long. Cut baby corn in half lengthwise. Cut squash into ½ inch cubes. Slice bamboo shoots lengthwise.

IN A WOK, heat peanut oil and fry shrimp for 1–2 minutes then remove. Add garlic, chile pepper, green onions, squash and snow peas, and fry for 1–2 minutes. Add stock and simmer for about 5 minutes. Add bamboo shoots and tomatoes and simmer for 1 minute. Stir in noodles and shrimp. Season to taste with soy and oyster sauce. Check seasoning and add salt and pepper, if needed.

GARNISH with cilantro and serve.

VEGETABLES

WOK COOKING AND VEGETABLES provide the perfect pairing of quick cooking with healthy eating. With their bright colors and crunchy texture, stir-fried vegetables can play a starring role in your menu or serve as healthy side dishes. The vegetable recipes are also easily adaptable to hearty non-vegetarian fare with the addition of meat or seafood, if you want to serve a more substantial dish.

Mixed Colorful Vegetables

12 dried shiitake mushrooms,
   drained and stems removed
1 stalk celery
2 medium carrots, peeled
¾ cup bean sprouts
4 tbs vegetable oil
1 clove garlic, minced
1 thumb-sized piece of ginger
   root, minced
4 green onions, chopped
2 small zucchini, sliced
1 red bell pepper, stems and
   seeds removed, and sliced
1 pinch sugar
3 tbs light Chinese
   soy sauce
2 tbs oyster sauce
1 small can bamboo shoots,
   drained and sliced
Kosher salt
Freshly ground pepper

SOAK SHIITAKES in warm water for 10–15 minutes. Cut celery and carrots into 1½ inch pieces and then into strips. Rinse bean sprouts and remove green pods that float to the top, then drain.

IN A WOK or large pan, heat vegetable oil and lightly brown garlic and ginger. Add vegetables and shiitakes and stir-fry over high heat for 4 minutes. Add a cup of hot water and cook for about 5 minutes. Season to taste with salt, pepper, sugar, soy sauce, and oyster sauce. Add bamboo shoots and bean sprouts to the wok and braise for about 3 more minutes.

SERVE WITH RICE, noodles, meat, or poultry dishes.

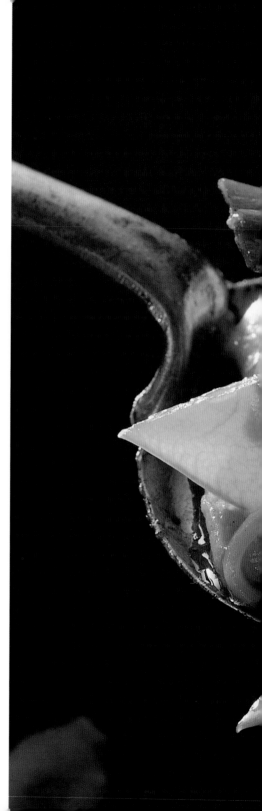

Savory Pineapple

1 fresh pineapple (about 2½ lb)

¼ cup light brown sugar, separated

1 tsp turmeric

3 green onions

2 fresh red serrano chile peppers,
    stem removed

3 tbs peanut oil

2 cloves garlic, minced

2 whole star anise

1 cinnamon stick

6 whole cloves

3 tbs fresh ginger root, peeled
    and minced

1 tsp salt

PEEL PINEAPPLE and remove any remaining "eyes." Cut into quarters, remove hard core, and cut into pieces of about ¾ inch. Place in a saucepan and sprinkle with 3 tablespoons of brown sugar and turmeric. Add just enough water to cover pineapple and simmer uncovered for 10 minutes. Drain pineapple and save liquid.

CHOP GREEN ONIONS into thin rings. Cut serrano chiles into rings.

IN A WOK or large pan, heat peanut oil and stir fry garlic, green onions, star anise, cinnamon stick, and cloves for 2 minutes. Add ginger, ⅓ cup of the saved pineapple liquid, salt and remaining brown sugar, and simmer for 3–4 minutes. Add chile peppers and pineapple and simmer for 3–4 minutes.

SERVE AS A SIDE DISH with pork, duck, or chicken.

Fried Tofu with Peanuts and Vegetables

1 lb firm tofu

1 tbs dark soy sauce

2 tbs light soy sauce

1 tsp cornstarch

⅓ lb unsalted raw peanuts

1 small red bell pepper, stems, seeds, and ribs removed

6–7 green onions

2 cups vegetable oil for deep-frying

2 fresh green serrano chile peppers, stems and seeds removed, and diced

1 tbs ginger root, peeled, minced, and sliced

2 cloves garlic, minced

1 tbs chopped garlic chives (Chinese chives)

Kosher salt

Seasoning sauce

¾ cup vegetable stock

1 tbs dark soy sauce

2 tbs light soy sauce

1 tsp white rice vinegar (5% acid)

1 tsp cornstarch

½ tsp Szechwan peppercorns

DRAIN AND PAT DRY TOFU, and cut into ¾ inch cubes. In a bowl, mix together dark and light soy sauce, salt, and cornstarch. Add tofu cubes, stir, cover, and marinate for 30 minutes.

REMOVE ANY BROWN SKINS from the peanuts. Cut red bell pepper into 1½ inch cubes. Cut green onions diagonally into ¾ inch pieces.

FOR THE SEASONING SAUCE: Whisk vegetable stock, soy sauces, vinegar, and cornstarch in a bowl. Finely crush peppercorns with the back of a heavy skillet and stir into sauce.

IN A WOK, heat vegetable oil to 355°F. Remove tofu from marinade, drain well, fry in batches for about 2 minutes until golden, and remove. Fry peanuts in the wok for 1 minute, remove, and drain.

REMOVE ALL but about 2 tablespoons oil and reheat. Add chile peppers, ginger and garlic, and stir-fry briefly. Add bell peppers and green onions and fry for 2 minutes. Add seasoning sauce and bring to a boil. Stir in tofu and peanuts and simmer for 1 minute. Transfer to plates, sprinkle with garlic chives, and serve immediately.

TIP

▶ Marinating and stir-frying with ginger and garlic turns tofu into a real delicacy. Accompany with fragrant basmati rice.
▶ Bean curd or tofu is one of the great achievements of Chinese cuisine and is also available in many forms in Thai markets.

Tasty Tofu and Vegetables

1½ lb firm tofu
1 tbs fresh ginger root, peeled
    and diced
4 tbs light soy sauce
5–6 dried cloud ear mushrooms
2–3 green onions
⅓ cup peanut oil
1 small red bell pepper, stems, seeds
    and ribs removed, and diced
¼ lb white mushrooms, cleaned
    and sliced
¼ lb shiitake mushrooms, stems
    removed and sliced
⅛ lb fresh enoki mushrooms,
    cleaned, stems, seeds and
    ribs removed, and sliced
½ lb cleaned baby spinach
Cooked rice

Sauce
1 tbs dark miso
4 tbs rice wine (sake)
4 tbs sweet rice wine (mirin)
2 tbs light soy sauce
½–¾ cup vegetable stock
1 dash lime juice

DRAIN AND PAT DRY TOFU and cut into cubes about ¾ inch cubes. In a bowl, combine tofu, ginger, and soy sauce. Stir and marinate for about 1 hour.

SOAK CLOUD EAR MUSHROOMS in lukewarm water for 15–20 minutes, drain well, and cut into strips. Chop green onions into fine rings.

FOR THE SAUCE: Combine miso, both types of rice wine, soy sauce, stock and lime juice, and set aside.

IN A WOK or large pan, heat peanut oil. Drain tofu well, pat dry, and save marinade. Add tofu to wok, fry until crispy (watch out for splattering oil), and remove. Remove all but 2 tablespoons of oil from the wok. Add green onions and bell peppers and fry for 2 minutes. Add mushrooms and spinach and fry for 1 minute. Pour in sauce and tofu marinade and simmer for 1 minute. Stir in tofu, heat, and add seasoning. Serve with rice.

Tri-Color Asian Vegetables

½ lb baby carrots

1 large celery stalk, cleaned

1 small young leek (about ¼ lb), cleaned and rinsed

⅓ lb green beans, ends removed

¼ lb cherry tomatoes, cores removed

¾ cup vegetable stock

2 tbs light soy sauce

1 tbs oyster sauce

2 tbs cashews

2 tbs peanut oil

1 fresh red serrano chile pepper, stem and seeds removed, and diced

1 clove garlic, minced

¼ tsp cornstarch

Cilantro for garnish

Kosher salt

Freshly ground pepper

CUT CARROTS lengthwise into halves or quarters. Remove any tough threads from celery with a vegetable peeler and cut into sticks 1½ inches long and ¼ inch wide matchsticks. Cut leek into pieces about 2 inches long and ½ inch wide. Cut beans in half crosswise. Cut cherry tomatoes in half crosswise.

COMBINE STOCK, soy sauce, oyster sauce, salt and pepper, and set aside.

IN A WOK, toast cashews briefly and remove.

IN A WOK or large pan, heat peanut oil and stir-fry chile pepper and garlic. Add carrots and beans and stir-fry for 2–3 minutes. Add celery and leeks and stir-fry for 1–2 minutes. Add seasoned stock and reduce heat to low. Cover and simmer for about 10 minutes until vegetables are just tender. For the last 2–3 minutes, add and simmer tomatoes. Stir cornstarch into a little water and use to thicken sauce. Add seasoning to taste.

TRANSFER TO SERVING PLATE, sprinkle with reserved cashews, and garnish with cilantro.

Zesty Stir-Fried Broccoli

1 large carrot, peeled
1 small celery stalk
1–2 fresh red serrano chile
    peppers, stems removed
1–2 green onions
3 tbs peanut oil
1 lb fresh broccoli florets, washed
    and dried
1 large red bell pepper, stems, seeds
    and ribs removed, and sliced
¾ cup vegetable stock, separated
1 tbs oyster sauce
2–3 tbs light soy sauce
¼ tsp cornstarch
Cooked rice
Kosher salt
Freshly ground pepper

CUT CARROT into ½ inch cubes. Clean celery and slice finely. Cut chile peppers into rings. Slice green onions into thin rings.

IN A WOK, heat peanut oil and stir-fry broccoli florets. Add bell peppers, carrots, celery, chile peppers and green onions, and fry briefly. Pour in ½ cup stock, season with salt and pepper, reduce heat, and cook for 5–8 minutes. Combine oyster sauce, soy sauce, remaining stock and cornstarch, pour into wok, stir, and bring to a boil. Season to taste with salt and pepper.

SERVE with rice.

Stir-Fried Choy Sum

½ lb choy sum or Chinese broccoli
1 small celery stalk
1 green onion
2 tbs peanut oil
½ small red bell pepper, stems and
    seeds removed, and diced
1 tbs fresh ginger, minced
1 clove garlic, minced
¼ cup canned bamboo shoots,
    drained and minced
½ cup shiitake mushrooms, stems
    removed and quartered
1 small fresh red serrano chile
    pepper, stems, seeds and ribs
    removed, and diced
2 tbs light soy sauce
1 tbs fish sauce
Grated peel from 1 kaffir lime
¼ lb small, cooked shrimp, peeled
1 tbs chopped cilantro
Kosher salt
Freshly crushed black peppercorns

RINSE CHOY SUM well and trim stalks, if stalks are thicker than ¼ inch, trim with a vegetable peeler. Blanch broccoli in boiling water for 1 minute. Remove from water and drain on towel to cool and dry. Slice broccoli leaves into ¼ inch wide ribbons. Slice broccoli stalks on the diagonal into ½ inch pieces. Cut celery into 2 inch strips. Chop white part of green onion and cut green part into rings.

IN A WOK, heat peanut oil, and lightly brown celery, bell peppers, ginger, and garlic. Stir in choy sum, bamboo shoots, shiitakes, green onion rings and chile pepper, and fry thoroughly. Season with soy sauce, fish sauce, salt, pepper, and lime peel. Add shrimp and toss briefly. Transfer to bowls and sprinkle with cilantro.

TIP

► Choy Sum, also known as Chinese flowering cabbage, is the finest tasting in its category, which also includes mustard spinach, Chinese broccoli, and bok choy. The best method for cooking this vegetable is stir-frying, which allows the cabbage, and especially the stems, to retain its crunchy structure and juicy core. The peppery hot aroma comes from the seasonings.

► Fresh from the market is sure to be the best quality so shop at farmers' markets for best variety and flavor.

► Vegetarian cooking and eating are really fun when you use top-quality products. In a pinch, you could leave out the shrimp, but they're excellent in this dish.

INDEX